W9-CDI-614

Play Day

The Sound of Long A

By Alice K. Flanagan

Today is play day.

Kay plays house
with Fay.

5

Ray plays with clay.

Kate plays
on skates.

10

James plays with games.

Shane plays with a toy train.

Tracy plays with her bird Casey.

15

Brady plays with his dog Lady.

18

Jamie plays with her pig Amy.

Can you name more boys and girls at play?

Word List:

Amy	James	plays
Brady	Jamie	Ray
Casey	Kate	Shane
clay	Kay	skates
day	Lady	today
Fay	name	Tracy
games	play	train

Note to Parents and Educators

The books in this series are based on current research, which supports the idea that our brains are pattern-detectors rather than rules-appliers. This means children learn to read easier when they are taught the familiar spelling patterns found in English. As children encounter more complex words, they have greater success in figuring out these words by using the spelling patterns.

Throughout the series, the texts provide the reader with the opportunity to practice and apply knowledge of the sounds in natural language. The books introduce sounds using familiar onsets and *rimes,* or spelling patterns, for reinforcement.

For example, the word *cat* might be used to present the short "a" sound, with the letter *c* being the onset and "_at" being the rime. This approach provides practice and reinforcement of the short "a" sound, as there are many familiar words made with the "_at" rime.

The stories and accompanying photographs in this series are based on time-honored concepts in children's literature: well-written, engaging texts and colorful, high-quality photographs combine to produce books that children want to read again and again.

Dr. Peg Ballard
Minnesota State University, Mankato

The Child's World®

childsworld.com

Published by The Child's World®
1980 Lookout Drive • Mankato, MN 56003-1705
800-599-READ • www.childsworld.com

ACKNOWLEDGMENTS

The Child's World®: Mary Berendes, Publishing Director
The Design Lab: Design
Michael Miller: Editing

PHOTO CREDITS

© Alena Ozerova/Shutterstock.com: 5; andresr/
iStockphoto.com: 18; in.focus/iStockphoto.com: 13;
hartcreations/iStockphoto.com: 17; JLBarranco/
iStockphoto.com: 14; kali9/iStockphoto.com: 21;
LivingImages/iStockphoto.com: 9; MariaBobrova/
iStockphoto.com: 6; Ronnachai Palas/Shutterstock.com:
cover, 2; stefansonn/Shutterstock.com: 10

ISBN 9781634070263
LCCN 2015930169

Printed in the United States of America
Mankato, MN
July, 2015
PA02267

ABOUT THE AUTHOR

Alice Flanagan lives with her husband in Chicago, Illinois, and writes books for children and teachers. Ever since she was a young girl, Ms. Flanagan has enjoyed writing. Today, she has more than 70 books published on a wide variety of topics. Some of the books she has written include biographies of U.S. presidents and first ladies; biographies of people working in our neighborhood; phonics books for beginning readers; informational books about birds; and career education in the classroom.